# COME CLOSER

# COME CLOSER

## Leanne Averbach

Tightrope Books

Tightrope Books
602 Markham Street
Toronto, Ontario
Canada M6G 2L8
www.TightropeBooks.com

**ONTARIO ARTS COUNCIL**
**CONSEIL DES ARTS DE L'ONTARIO**

Edited by Roo Borson.
Copyedited by Shirarose Wilensky.
Cover design by Karen Correia Da Silva.
Typesetting by Shirarose Wilensky.
Camera illustrations by Rod Hunting.

**Canada Council**
**for the Arts**

**Conseil des Arts**
**du Canada**

Produced with the assistance of the Canada Council for the Arts and the Ontario Arts Council.

Printed in Canada.

LIBRARY AND ARCHIVES CANADA CATALOGUING IN PUBLICATION

Averbach, Leanne
    Come closer / Leanne Averbach.

Poems.
ISBN 978-1-926639-19-2

    I. Title.


PS8601.V46C66 2010        C811'.6        C2010-902914-3

# TABLE OF CONTENTS

## ONE

## TWO

# THREE

# FOUR

# FIVE

SIX

# ONE

## A THING PAST

may be plucked of a sudden from the well, its memory
cavity. No query is necessary, nor forwarding address.

It may arrive dull, meaningless, slathered in vague clutter,
or rise pristine to quake us, better

than ever from nowhere. It will peel us raw
in a flash—that muted ransom. It repeats, no will to resist,

harnessing us to the bed. It has a keen sense
of smell and fashion. It remembers a friend

of a friend who knew all about the incident. It is a witness
who doesn't show up as you make the case again, again the indefinite

verdict, an urge to call someone. *Hello? Am I okay?* Ruby cascades
of elixir in your glass help alternately to hold it, send it back into the well, create

new files in which to keep it. That awkward taste of the half-
learned, the feel of being tattooed inside, an extra set of organs

for recalling. Out the window Canada Geese point elsewhere,
passports in their brains. They take one last look at themselves

in the lagoon before slipping off the radar as gulls scratch
the air, bragging winter-worthiness

through rubbery feathersuits and I drift
beneath the shadowy flim-flam of love.

# SPEAKING IN THE VENTRICULAR

My heart is hair
Teased, bouffant
Convertible swept
Back and forth

My heart is bottle
Vitreous, Molotov
A substitute vase, a ship
Rolled up, a note

My heart is history
Repetitive, loaded
My heart is horse
It knows the way back

My heart is money
Though it won't play
My heart is pistol
It smokes, then hides away

# MY YOUTH MACHINE-ROLLED, SMOKED TO ITS STUB

Tales of my youth are a big hit at parties.

The arrest—cops cleaving
me to their sedan.
Caught red-handed, skin
of newsprint bearing the image
of a living Mao
laid tenderly
on a metal pole.
Then the cell, its plain cavity.
The beefy women in uniform
watching me bathe
through a slit.

I forget to mention
the bulb that buzzed
above the narrow cell cot
shredding my brain
into a bell jar
of worms, the best of them
lacking all conviction.
Or a ceiling stain the shape
of a slow sob.

Outside the prison gates, headlines
waited like friends who knew me
as a child: "Comrade _____
Valiantly Defies Fascist Police . . ."
and so on. The quicksand
of celebrity, how important
I must be. The next 8 years
a fugue of factory jobs,
the Chairman's words, a chain
of smokes in my pocket.

Decades later, Mao's
personal physician reported
the Chairman had enjoyed
after a dip in the Yangtse to bathe
in the vaginal fluids of virgins.
He shared with Marlon Brando
a grotesque eating disorder, and a taste
for servile foreign women. I had always
liked Marlon, too; his sensitive mouth.

# A TOOL I CAN SAY WITH

The park today is warm-leafed. Buttery and bloodorange.
While bands of canines walk their men, teaching grace and tolerance
for the sake of a good run at freedom, I too could be considering a fall
in season. I have lots of thin tragedy to complain of,
lost again in the pathways though I've travelled often.
Me with my tamped wildness, doodling like a painter
with a spear, fight turning to bloodletting within.
Almost a real old girl, my blood now boils
lunch onto my hips. Too old
to be miserable; or happiness is too young
for me—that insipid injustice. I don't know.
But I just feel good. Fetching a stick in my teeth
and, drooling and panting, handing it to you
in this luminous November park
is an act I could feel proud of, a gesture
worthy of our love.

# CHANGING CHANNELS

*2007*

Summer is a mild racket.
Twenty-four-hour news seeps

through mesh into oversweet air.
Like legions of crickets

rubbing statistics from their tiny wings,
wanting not to disturb

our scrim of little miseries. There's your lover
waiting for you to think more of him.

He is your Penelope. He can pierce the airborne
world, fill the empty bow. There's the list:

case of beer, fishing pole, drowning
lake, closed since the fish stopped.

The cricket's chirp is generated by raising
a forewing, rubbing it against the staggering calm.

This stridulating sound is also called
brain quiet. Here on the western front.

# SLIM EVIDENCE OF DUBIOUS QUALITY

*December 2008*

I've never bought into the whole body as temple thing.
Of course, I want to live and love.
Breakfast this morning with its monster yellow eyes
is just drugs in the food chain playing tricks; my mind is good.
Yesterday I had a small lesion removed, age stuff,
nothing scary. Okay, the truth: a vanity issue.
The man with the laser went at me
numerous times and I had to cry "Stop!"
for a second or two; I wanted to strangle him.
Just now I read five detainees
in Guantanamo, originally from Algeria, like Camus
if I am not mistaken—a scalding yellow-eyed irony there—
will be released from their unlawful imprisonment
based on slim evidence for the last seven years.
The buildings of the compound have thick
soundproof walls. When darkness falls
the guards speak to one another of a terrible
boredom. None of the staff has been
strangled, so far as I know.

# 9-1-1

Here as you know is the socket
of her eye. An overfull bowl
flecked and reflecting
you, darkly. The soldier
somehow home. In Mosul,
slag pelted the hyacinths, melted
the houses, hardened
inside your fist, your
Bragg boy chest.
Shaken through hell
you are empty and opaque
and to swing at her was a mistake.
A question waiting to pop.
A question now slumped in the corner
with someone's children.
Broken you, still on duty.
Laughing tracks of a civilization blare
from the TV and your wife's eye
is a bloody carpet, her lid jammy
and defeated: a win
of sorts, she's down.
Here, as you know,
is the other orb, locked on you
and ancient; it dares you,
wink, wink. Because you know
how it ends and you know something
can end. She's dialing.

# TASTE OF CITY

He swings from machine to curb like Gene Kelly—one swing down
into the slouch, a day's garbage lining the narrow street.

He is our Prince of Forgetting. His gloves and clothing are the colour
of whipped trash, his hair fatty and dull. He feeds the ass of the truck, its ripe

jaws dripping mouthfuls of New York. My cherry VW is more crimson
in the sun, my coffee is slung in its tray, iced, safe as a baby.

The man feels me following his moves, the ooze, and the August heat
stinks of rodent breath. He slows to the carp of cars behind

to look in at me and his mouth puckers too tightly, my teeth
find lip. Anything plays on the radio, and noon sun strikes

through the pane dividing us
onto my bare summer legs.

# UNSEXY

A genuine surprise in bed
last night while reading a poem
by Frank O'Hara, something about
destroying another's idea of himself
in order to seduce him, reminded me how
unsexy sex can be. Like in '69 I was selling
flowers in nightclubs, having dropped
out, university seemed so pointless, and
I remember this one bar where the floors
were sticky everything was sticky and nothing
stuck to the women on the platforms in cages and
it was welfare cheque day and one guy with a sort of
rotting face looked at me wistfully, said *Here* and handed
me 20 dollars for a rose. But then later at a very happening
venue a guy with a manicure waited for the nickel
back on a 95 cent flower, and afterwards, in the company
van, we dropout flowerchicks got high on the boss's
smoke to laugh off the feel of all the men and the world
of men, and the boss whipped out his
dick. Memorable too was a man when I was 10
he invited me into the bushes to see his
underpants. I remember how nice he seemed
so much sadder than my crazy Aunt Rose who got married
at fifteen with a brown suitcase and rules for spitting
at the evil eye and she spat when I tried to tell her
about the underpants you see she was watching me

while my parents were in Vegas watching
showgirls, probably in cages. I think it must have been
even earlier my friend and I were torturing my little cousin
in the basement took off all her clothes and wrote
on her, perhaps my first lines, with all the lipstick
from our mothers' vanities when the phone rang
it was my Aunt Dora calling little cousin
home for dinner and my poetry
was published, and to this day I never feel anything
I write is ready. Much later I remember friends
visiting, and my ex-husband's large balls,
when he was still my husband, sort of
peeking from his summer shorts like kiwis
growing in Canada when he crossed those great
legs, and my feeling disgust and pride both
like a full-blown argument for later
therapy court, why I had stuck it out
so long. And then that hypnotherapist
in '86 who wanted me to act it all out with
feeling, proponent of the Lee Strasberg
School of Behavioural Psychology that
he was, twice a week for a month or
two, just the two of us, on his lush
and he thought irresistible
Persian rug.

# SORRY

Done well, loss can feel somehow satisfying—
the cheap vase dropped, the guarded inheritance

finally liberated. But sloppy loss makes losing
prickly. The upended table

after an argument, great cheesecake
on someone's Gucci this or that

or the very popular electronic trail
of a password once shared

to buy a book. Then the note
found in its erotic

entirety—the discovery
that passion often wants

to transcribe itself—and some time
later, a speech

delivered over twisty cocktails and nuts,
and numerous costume changes

by the drunk and devoted
dresser who works the brain.

TWO

# PSORIASIS

Everyone I know is about my skin
condition sympathetic. I'm a moulter

from my hands feet and scalp,
as my father was before me and

like many fine beasts in the kingdom,
but I get the pleasure all year round.

Deposits of my skin trail me
like someone horribly lost

who as they search for a way out
of it all, wants to be found.

Growing old alone is a shock.
I apparently have a knack for solitude

or the other way around.
I started out mad

for the roller coaster.
It taught me ups and downs

last only a few brief moments.
Bumper cars really rocked

when I didn't get a dud. An education
of sorts, for gamblers and brats

of my generation; not
very helpful for being

me. Now my heart
has lost its carmine candy

coating. Anyone can take a bite.
And my skin grows thinner and

it wants me to let go. I've grown fond
of winter, its justifiable furs.

When the furnace goes, as it has
often this season, I can play

Cavewoman. I warm my hands
on the pictures drawn

on the television and await
the birth of Fire.

# THE TV NEWSMEN WHO LIVE IN DESIGNER THROATS

The TV newsmen who live in designer throats
and skinny-hipped polls they knit themselves
all for me, for me seek positive glints
in stacks of war—such handsome, shockproof eyes!—
find sudden criminals on untroubled streets and
take saline counts in politicians' cries.
360 degrees, 24 hours, my! They are my picket-
toothed, my constants, my porticoes, my
defence. But why, too, the staccato, near
palimpsest of commercial breaks? Well, naturally,
my dew-kissed anchors & pundits with couturier throats
need rest; the rest of us need buy
and buy—the Moon, dead and pretty
in the farrago sky.

# A BRIEF HISTORY OF THE BLUES

Clifford Gibson had musical teeth.
He polished them & they lit Blind

Blake's obscurity up—then both were gone.
William Moore, a barber by trade, cut

eight extant songs and Peg Leg
Howell did crazy things with his one

hit. Blind Willie J's bottleneck howled
"Dark Was the Night (Cold Was the Ground)"

though his contented wife disagreed. Blind Lemon
Jefferson died mysteriously almost

famous, but not before igniting Ramblin'
Thomas. His big brother, Babyface T

& his Jug Band blew actual fat
bottles—there's a sound movie somewhere.

Presciently, you might say, the Sheiks
from Mississippi wrote "Sitting on Top

of the World." One of the sheiks, Skip
James, said unequivocally

"I'm So Glad" and rockers The Cream
much later repeated it. Bo Weavil

Jackson just wanted to say
"You Can't Keep No Brown"

and his frenetic masterpiece did.
Furry Lewis got his edge from

Blind Joe who later met Burt Reynolds and
Blind Willie McTell inspired Sam Collins

or the other way around.
Blind Carey Davis & Blind Boy Fuller

were protégés, a case of no blind
leading. It's said the drive

and hokum style of Papa
Charlie Jackson did "Shake

That Thing" though Buddy Boy
Hawkins' raggy repertoire impeccably

faded into obscurity.
Sluefoot Joe gave music

up for the pulpit, Depression

style, whereas preachin' Son House

gave God back, and Muddy
Waters was glad. Sweet Blind Willie

McTell had a sweet wife Kate and
Mississippi John Hurt was a three-finger

picker. The fleeting falsetto of Peetie
Wheatstraw was felled fatally in a car.

# DANCES OF THE 1960s

Dogs in moonlit coats lope in packs past Cadillacs, unleashed
as dogs once were, over asphalt, lawns plush and sprung, airy
as dance floors. My breath turns with theirs in the neat streets—a run
towards my first Boy. I am new, dangerous. I will debunk polyester
and pearls, prove youth maligned. Travel far from ugliness, glitter
of betterment. Away from Fathers, all sweat and money, faltering
inside their cocktails of verve while their wives dream
of other men—Kirk Douglas leaping Odyssean, teaching them
about biceps and the red relationship between wine and feet.
I am mini-skirted and bold. The stage is waiting.
Canine breath pumps atmospheric around the infinite future.

# IN GRAND CENTRAL STATION HE SAT DOWN & WEPT

The morning wind is up as fabulous
footwear leaps into stairwells and his cup
is empty as a lemming's pocket.

His heavens are hemmed.
His America heavy, and in a foul mood.

The leaner noonday throng, the odd Could Be
Me Tomorrow, is the septum punch he needs
and his finances are briefly more excellent.
His stomach flowers a sore of nostalgia.

This must all be a mistake.

A 2:28 coin comes in for a landing on the matching tarmacs
of his palms. God bless. It is a discus of laughing nickel.

Market Close is always a ringing of inconceivable love.
His mouth pulls festively on a free coffee.
Tides of overcoat are coming every which gate; he's ready.
Just as he was before his mind grew an
eye always on the McDonald's trash can.

Behold the roar of multiple money, as if it recalls him.

# BAGGAGE CLAIM

No, that's not it. Mine has a metallic flap
concealing the heart of the bag.
An old bag, richly banged
up and down countless stairways
promising then relinquishing heaven. No,
that's not it either. How amazing, though:
from the farthest curve of the carousel
to make the positive ID, a tiny tag or blood
stain where you and I tried once again
to tandem the journey. There,
swinging into view. All of this moment's
possessions, circling amongst the black
grieving clones, gliding towards me.
My silver bullet, my unmistakable exit
in distinctive, flexible casing,
getting close—But now, look,
it's an unlucky warrior, innards flowing
out through a crack in the armour.
A swath of my lace nightie snags
the turnstile, preening with it the bra
of flowered satin you might have
given me early on, and
I notice a man, or a few, slipping me in
or out of the garments, as the whole
turning machine brakes
to a long painful scream.

Halted before me, my sliver bag stares
exposed like a Medieval cross-dresser.
The crowd cheers as I pull
my wreckage away, simply,
an animal looking to bury it.

# REPLICA

The rain-rotted brown hold-out
of a house below
this field of high-rises,
down there, out my high city
-sooted window, my wanting
to look out at all
costs, not in, at this crimped
paradise that was
a marriage—it's exactly
that old house, it is.

It's the fool
of a gull straddling the rotting
peak of shake shingle with her fat orange feet,
waddling towards the back of a crow that
arrived there first, his Rorschach of black, his raven
pointyness twitching at the possibilities
of bird in this January dusk.

And the buckling asphalt
way down there
where street and alley meet
overflowing deranged rivulets of rain;
is that our noir, too?
Did the workers break for beer
just there, and return to roll

out the asphalt with random
strokes, a sloppy liquid
lunch turned solid hell
surface now for boarders and bladers,
the elderly, the loveless?

# DARWIN IS DESPONDENT

I understand the billboard's promise.
I get the spire, but not the spirit.
I hear the troops get pizza.
I understand a little Texan.

I've considered everyone knows
          two, forbids zero, attempts three.
And I do appreciate you've conducted
          a comprehensive search outside
          and in this luminous dress.

I understand the lozenge is the
          moon, the tree an altar. And the red peignoir
          rustling is the sound of all this classifying.

You come from away. I understand you can't stay.
Even the finch, after such a contribution, was misunderstood.

# TO THE LIGHTHOUSE

### I. THE WINDOW

The sun up to its lips in sky    Woolf lists waves    A frame shivering
lace    (Here she refers to a series of echoes)    The wide lawn veined
with tree    Our frail bark    And he stood by the urn as a point
on the terrace    The Lost Scholar    She thought (a common
illness  See: *S. Freud*)    The strange equation marriage    Catenates
the mind    Never did anyone look so    Mothers, sons, a summer
house    Perfect empty tide    to the lighthouse

### II. TIME PASSES

Now the question of the ten years    Her *Outline* reads:  Dissolution,
gradual everything    The War    Women cleaning oblivion up
We are handed children    The devouring accumulates
Son "lost" in war    She slept life

### III. THE LIGHTHOUSE

The living son steers to lighthouse with Father, "his scholar fence of
sanctity"    See *Moments of Being* pp. 40-41    (On shore watching
them, an attitude of easel)    Another sun up to its lips in blue
As after a long illness, bomb-vivid    Where the moment (threw out
like radium)    Very Woolf, this robe of flesh    (Artist thinks
from shore:   Why create?    Canvas to end beneath sofa
And marriage, a slipper dangling from its famous foot)

The boat drowses in the bay    Father, son, sandwiches,
silence and so on    Then crinolines of sea
Wave-smashing light creasing rock    The beach, now
the lighthouse, its quick white shape    It was one's body
The flourishing centre    The already half out of the picture
She will later paint a trail "Intolerable"    (There is evidence
of condensing here)  Some gash in the lousy sea    Some bed
in the wood    Some essays, room, and so on

# BIG

The tallest man ever was
an American.
Robert Pershing Wadlow
of Illinois, 7 foot 8
at the age of five and
later 8 foot 8 at twenty-two,
died alone in his sky.

According to some
Hebrew chroniclers, Goliath
of Gath stood at 9 ½ feet
but Flavius Josephus' translations
of the Septuagint offer the more
credible 6 foot 10.

Much later French anthropometrist
Paul Topinard could not pull
off his tallest man of Finland
claim, nor could a drum major
in the Russian Imperial Regiment—
femurs and tibias in Leiden Museum
display the lucent truth.

Last night I measured you
beneath a tall ambergris
moon, fragrant and ash-
coloured, in the calipers
of my gaze.

You were no giant,
no Ringling acromegalith
tightrope-walking out that door.
I recalled the celebrated midget
Jozef ("Count") Boruwlaski
of Poland, a mere 35 inches
at his peak. How his memory,
past all expectation, lived on.

# THE INVENTION OF PORNOGRAPHY

To paint and sculpt them was severely
punished. Parisian printers, less regulated,

provided sodomites, whores, horny soon-
famed protagonists, uncourtly twin aristocrats
and clerics with skirt and codpiece billowing

upward. The visual scandals—a culture
arose. The entire act of seeing took fresh tint

as Marie & Louis eyed the royal blood-bottom
of a bucket. But more the uncontrollable had
unleashed: intersection, collision—nodes

of the erotic, oceans of tumescence, itself
the end. Right up into this: our capsized

little study group on a purple-petalled
afternoon, spread wide in your
garden—its leaf-split summer light.

# LET'S GET LOST

*New York City, 2005*

Look, it's Chet Baker
all mooding black and white

in a photo beneath an eyebrow
of plaster in Café Loup.

There was big sound
climbing out of the tunnel

under the Hudson tonight, buoys punctuating
above like drunken ellipses,

and those benches lining the boardwalk
are designed for no rest.

So I'm here with Chet being
bloosy when the barman

says the stage can be dark
as a heart and Rilke

was also afraid. Gagged
in the black-and-white dagues

on the whitewashed wall over there
more friends: Dorothy flaming

Parker just a Matisse away
from Marlene Dietrich, open

on a bench of satin with an elliptic river
of velvety boys, androids

from another era, but forgive me,
your name? It escapes

as I am flanked by an all-overness,
a going back and returning. I mean,

earlier under gibbous moons
on the river I felt like an armature

for heroic gesture; you know,
a spinning entropic thing

with obdurate, blazing heels.
Come closer. You have that

undetonated look—
nowhere as a cul-de-sac.

I must tell you: earlier,
riverlit, slung wide

as a Marlene
on the boardwalk

the sky was cocked
on my head just so.

Sense was away. I was
smoulder, and fear

was having a lie-down,
aging in her sleep.

# THREE

## PIGEON

Lousy bird with your ashen hair. What balcony
        dreams have you today?

To defile my paltry rectangle of escape
        no doubt.

Fecund stylist, go away.
                Leave yourself less near me. Amsterdam

is an avenue of avian plenty and I see your flick-eyed lust. Go,
        scat, leave me to my puny New York

terrace, my minor afternoon
                catastrophe, and I'll offer this counsel:

        in love, tilt not thy tail
            for any Abelard.

        No common, devout, and handsome dove
            or garbage ripper.

        In short, be trashy
                but be choosey.

# PROJECTION

A woman is fondling her cello on the flat nebulae
of this gummy subway stage. It's July and I'm guessing
that guy over there, dampening inside his polo shirt, is thinking
      to blow town, office, stunt of pew—

it's on his demimonde look away—from
an earlier crimson hour perhaps, a woman's
sunburnt hands with bitten nail-tips, frayed as crayons in her lap
      and maybe there were songs

throbbing, car radios telling of their worsening situation? It's fun
to think about the sad secrecies of others while a musician fondles her cello
into the rotten underground air, and an empty train screams past us, hopefully
fast,
      towards repair.

# L - T R A I N

Above us the world
is typical. Here, things
rumble as a rat plays

chicken on the rails
and from your neck
hangs nevertheless

one of the gods.
The train screams in
to our rewind

of the past, designs
for what's next; in
to the loaded distraction

of waiting denizens
replete with sound
track. Though my hand

has misplaced yours
we are both in love
with the musician

as people eye with superb
inattention the malaise,
why, its veldt pause.

# TRANS CANADA DROWNING, SUMMER '96

—Out of the melting highway, a rest stop
yields right, friendly as a psychologist. Unsticking
from upholstery we emerge, swathed in a reeking
        silence.

With leftover bread, a little cheese
in a carworn manila bag we go down a path past
a map of where we are nothing
        beneath the capped arêtes of the Rockies.

Down, we amble down
to water's edge. You crouch, scoop up stones, drench
your hands and we both say *bleeding* of the slow-
marbled stone shades. And the bank crackles
        with geology.

Meaning to listen, we see
a big ghoulish bird perched implausibly on a
        sleek midstream boulder.

Its slate beak is clamped
around a damp manila sack of bread,
a little cheese, our last meal, freezing runoff
        coursing past.

# BEACHED

You are my frontispiece
while I read, onanize
with the classics.
Friends turn to Buddhism;
I turn you.

Long ago I fled, left you beneath low
lemon sun like a goblet on a towel, upended
and spilt in the sand on some cool Vancouver shore.

Youth has the wingspan of pterodactyls—
a bony useless confidence.
And I grow old in places I watched being born.
Glinting briefly, as if waiting for something real.

# VENICE

Pigeons roil in San Marco Square,
civilization filling their little heads,
as Viennese quartets play Bach and
Broadway to eight-dollar *tazze di caffe.*

And the mirrored boat is gliding us
backwards. Encrusted palaces, ochre
and pink, rise candylike from the fouled
canals. An elegant man on *Ponte del Rialto*

gazes down through us, one hand swimming
inside the shirt of a small boy pressed
in front of him, his other round the throat
of a marvelous woman: a family, Venice

in their eyes. Like a boa engorged with
traffic, the Grand Canal is dying
its gorgeous death and
entreats us: *Stay, forget your own.*

Outside the Naval Museum Molly
from Manchester carps about
tour service, the lion of Venice
reclining on her sensible sunhat.

Venice, zenith of man.
Invasion swells canals,
and gondoliers like arthropods
skate the fetid dollars.

# CUBA, POR FIN!

*2005*

The roads from Havana
scrawl into unscripted
distance. Frond
paradise, and no ideas
on what to buy, oh my.

Cars flirt
and colourize, forever
once young.
Who has not wanted
it: to still a time, our truest.

But we know this is a poor idea;
with the true comes
the all-too-true, though in Cuba—
what a soundtrack!
Cuba, I love your rhythms, your Che

dolls, your sanguine
Fidelity, your art
naive. I love you most
when I leave.
And return to nothing

averse. I wrap for you
the cocoa and the DVDs
and the dollars and recall the breeze
as the Malecon wall is wanked
by the irresistible, the sea.

# QUALICUM BEACH

*1980*

*for my son, Joseph*

Difficult to make a sentence
from catastrophe

> we know this from those screamless
> screaming dreams

& the skin leaves my son's hands
like chewing gum
to sizzle on the stove.

Angled for evening, the July sun
probes the grounds with me, searches
summer cottages
       for a doctor.

*Spread his hands* orders the medical man
       with mustard on his shirt
meaning the two peeled things
straining to claw at each other
as though angry at one another for exploring
where so much good food had come from
where mama spent too long looking away.

*Hold them tight* shouts the bandaging man
the four walls scraping with screams.

We were always in such a hurry then.
The imminence of some revolution
swaddling us like hair shirts.

Sometimes I see going back into
that night, taking the time
to lift the crisps of skin
off the iron stove plate
and burying them
tenderly like a set of foreskins
beneath lush Vancouver
Island poplars.

# MEDITATIONS ACROSS THE TABLE

I want to lounge between your lips, be your
cigarette, lie among their Real-Men-

Are-Complicated ways. Real men
are complicated, and I am recalling

a cold-war torture room with the bedroom
glances of Yves Montand

in *The Confession* (1970),
or how when Derrida died last week they said

in some nasty piece of obit news he was a fake
because deconstructing has no pattern, just eclectic

views. I could necromance all night
with lips like those and you

don't even smoke. I want you to
smoulder in my cell, confess every

thing, be my Boris *and* my personal
Baryshnikov, high over the alcove

of my ventricular, my chiaroscuro
hypothalamus in particular. I'll be

your projector your inspector
your Natasha or your Nancy in a Chevy

and we'll drive far past Delancey
'neath a starry geodesic night and

together we shall banquet
on indifference (your disguise).

Oh, let me clean you in some carwash
sponge away your past

identity, and hell, boy,
just ask: I'll be your KGB.

I'll wind you like some celluloid, eclipse
the glare the news

of who the good guys, who the sad,
just *Come on*—let my lips

be your one-and-only bona fide
weapons of induction.

FOUR

# ENTER THE CHUDNOVSKY BROTHERS

who insist they are functionally one
mathematician. One mind
having a crack

at digitizing a masterpiece:
the *Unicorn Tapestries*
from Brussels or Liege of 1500,

now in Manhattan Cloisters,
spun for a person
Unknown. The weft and warp

had liquefied
when the work was bathed,
time's stain removed, and now

the photo puzzle will not join—
a Frankenstein version
like the brothers themselves

whose threads of thought twist
ineluctably. Under fluorescence
they work as weavers, generally

men like themselves,
wove by daylight.
*The tapestry is like water*

says one brother into a lens.
*Water has no permanent*
*shape* says the other as a flare

of light from the door disturbs
the camera's eye examining
a wound—pomegranate

dye bleeding as blood
from the beloved and
captured Unicorn.

Mathematics swirl and swoop
for yards around the laboratory's
greaseboard floors, which

the brothers use when
the walls are full, to calculate
in unison.

Until Chudnovsky
and Chudnovsky admit
the gilded threads of the unicorn

in gardens of oxlip
bistort cuckoopint English bluebells
and Madonna lily

glisten into the world
beyond walls
and cannot be caught.

# POSTER CHILD

*1974*

Mao, cherubic poster
boy, buffed

and plastic as a product
rep must be, or Lenin

with his red-black
screed, that proletarian

glare—it all gave me
the fever.

Stovetop brews of glue
steamed and slavered

from buckets
onto my steel-toed boots

as I smeared
my handsome leaders

onto any clapboard, grimy pole.
Danger strobed like a party

for police, who sidled up, sent me
to the ground, and the sour odor

of steel bars malingering
in the cruiser's split-open

worn back seat hangs on
in me still. Along with my *Death*

*to Fascism,* their *Slut-bitch Commie,*
the *What kinda foreign name you got*

*there, Cunt,* and at the station the toothpaste
up the ass, the vibrant colonies

of lice, the howling
females, and how

"the screws"
really screw.

Now, Mao
decades dead,

no fever schools
of thought contend

within. There is danger
of rain tonight. Street lamps

unblinking as apparatchiks
shadow me and you

across the pavement and
onto the poster

idiots of advertisement
on the wall behind.

We dive into your
car where the dialectic

is hot and vinyl.
Interpretations vary.

# FEELING LUCKY

She was thin as a card.
He felt hungry and cooked inside.

He pulsed his morning neck but this back-fired;
his scent *Obélisque pour Hommes*

made her sneeze. He was rich, he was cartridge
but she was carriage and would not *ping!*

He looked at her lucky like
he'd found his MetroCard

but she was used up. *That is my final
copy*, she said in one ribbon of noir.

Because she was petroleum, he was scum on puddle.
Because she was fine as a heron lifting off.

## WAITING

In the bar, jazz—
its fast nothing.
A man yanks
at his tie, twists
a damp neck.
With him
his wristwatch
continues its
spindly goosestep.
Alone with child,
a woman, staring
so loudly out
at the evening she
may scream. Persian
carpet busies itself
underfoot, laced
with interlocking
patterns; a trick
track for the
eye, deranged
routes nowhere.
The bartender
quarrels with
himself over his
future & beneath
limp hoods

of disaffection a
couple stirs
their special whiskey
dystopic: sad cream
drizzling, elated
umbrellas above.

# MÜNCH IN MINIATURE

An unsteady city
bird, albino and jelly-eyed,
staggers on the parapet
yet the church clongs on oblivious.
The wind's mean, it's going at the skin
of the disrobed trees, and steel-crimson
clouds, birthmarks on night's
arriving, resist. Like old beards
igniting. One holds against the bluster
like the crest of a family line coming
to an end, and dusk burns upwards briefly.

The view from earth is the wind has torn
a thin round line of wonder from my
face, here on the eleventh
floor while I think: nameless
is this separation between us,
you still at the table wishing I'd stay.

# SAFFRON

The filaments of orange-yellow
on our plates, he says, are the pistils
of autumn crocuses
        picked, one-by-one, by hand

and we all inhale the fresh
trivia, stroke our rare
        thinning hair and try to imagine it:

fingers tweezing into the eye of the crocus,
a field of backs bent, curved
        as the things themselves

and the yellow fingertips,
young women fading
        like paper in the sun.

The image quavers
briefly in the heat of our eating,
        distant, Iberian

where we must go
some day, she says, a splinter
        of orange-yellow at rest

in her mouth and her mind
conjures a Spaniard, a wine
          and the perfect skirt.

# A PERFECT STAGE

Night is lately
a body unwilling to leave
things to themselves.
Each bothers each.
The day then at last rolls shut,
desk-like, indifferent to love.
Here's the liquid descent, quick
as a drain. At morning, there is whatever
can be held in senseless hands.
A dream, tiny lakes on dying planets
of memory, one famous
with your name. Another
is aflame as only dreams
can turn any substance
into me. Poultices of doubt
pock the surface of things.
Like a woman with leprosy
in biblical Hollywood
faced with God or banishment.
Simply, waking is a dropped call.
A keystone gone, the arch collapsed
into the glare of entrance.
The past now relearns its lines, seeking
the perfect stage for our story.
Even I want to hear it again.
How we failed the tests engraved

in our useless heads.
The weather reports it, sighing
through town—bags of plastic
thrown upwards, spectral
skins of desire.

# ROWING LESSON #9: GETTING OUT OF BED

From the wharf of linen
my live-in coxswain

prepares my team of limbs
with her cry, *Ready,*

to square their red-faced
joints, steady the beam

of my old shell with her
hands on my clackers,

to perk the hinged fin
of my rudder

for action. I grip
the shaft-ends of shallow

murk and dream
and drive them

with a catch
and a long sweep

in, in, in, abrading
the lit dawn.

# LATE GOOD GIRLS

Dad said, *Children, they hurt you.*
People did a lot of disowning in those days.
The way they saw it:

your boyfriend threw the pink Cadillac
keys back at them, abducting you, their first daughter.
Glammy Mom starved, took her Sleeping Stuff, nightlamp on.

She'd read, smoking Benson & Hedges
between monogrammed sheets as the drug seeped through her.
She was skinny as a herringbone. No name for it then.

Next, Dad and I,
letting the firemen in;
Mom in a slump, flirting.

Dad could sell you
the shirt off your back. Mom was
the brains though, capital B.

The way lamé behaved on her;
Mr. R. would slip in from the back lane,
Dad still at the store.

Dad'd glare at us
overtop those glasses!
Always looking for trouble.

Sisters: 1. It was like, *You can't disown me, Dad.*
       2. Hah! It was like, *I quit, Dad!*
But we each came back. Late good girls.

We got it: how they stuck bayonets where Dad
was hiding. Under the bed, his *shtetl* burning.
At Ellis Island his father shit his pants, ran back

onto the boat. A kid of seven—in charge
of parents and sisters in Canada!
A dollar in his boy's shoe.

They never talked in English
about before. The year Dad died, he blabbed
and blabbed. Let the camera roll.

FIVE

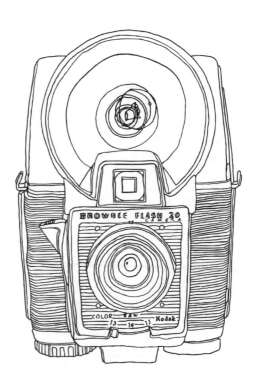

## TEACUPS & MINK

*Mama was a slim blonde*
*in T-bird convertibles, and*
*Dad perspired in plaid*
*suits the days of a big sale.*

*Basha and Lou were the old world*
*to new. They gave me this . . .*

## I.   TCHERNOVKA, GOODBYE

Tchernovka burning. Bayonets pointing
them towards Romania, into icy gusts
of hope. Through February windshriek

a knot of people claws west, the howl
hiding the clatter of things sewn into
coats, hems ploughing behind.

## II.   ENCOUNTER

A boy of seven among them
hears his auntie making animal
sounds, till he pulls her up onto his

narrow back, up to a lit
shack and a charred stone
hearth. And this is where

they met, Louie and his future
wife, first cousin Basha,
her new hot-hazel eyes

like earth eyes blazing
up at him, through all
the months of hems telling

in the snow. It was
his first lucky day
since he shook beneath

his bed, the smell of
horsemen, torches, his *shtetl*
burning. There he dreamed

up a doorway to Hymie
the butcher's shop where death
was just a sign of a meal to come

or to his Uncle Moyshe's who wore spats and
to avoid the army had his trigger finger
lopped off—Moyshe always had a great idea.

But the floor didn't open, fear stayed
shut in his belly, penned in like a wild horse
or White Russian horseman in the tavern afterwards.

And when the quiet weeping from his mother and sisters,
and the stench from his father's pants drew him out,
it was 1921. Tchernovka, Goodbye.

## III.  ESCAPE

As one they sailed to Canada
and with shrewd Diaspora feet
splintered into the swarm of Others

upon her shores, split
like a dropped vial
of mercury, or blood

and Louie gripped his parents'
damp hands, slid off a train into
icy London, Ontario, and they ran

out of money fast, a dollar in his boy's shoe.
But Moyshe and Bubba and baby Basha
wouldn't get off that train

till Vancouver, till Tchernovka
was half the world away—that Moyshe,
he always had a great idea.

Astride a horse and buggy,
Moyshe sold junk, sold the story
of his finger when he could.

# IV.   BANANAS IN CANADA

In London Beryl & Nellie clung
mute to their chairs so long
Louie left school, a torture

for the Yid Kid who was good at numbers, bad
at taking a finger in the eye, a smear of ice cream
in his face, or anything with words.

Thin soup, raggy coat, and mittens. Out went Louie
before frozen dawn to hawk newspapers, Louie the Hope,
penny upon penny, towers of pennies tall as a headed

chicken, so the soup got better. One day the miracle
of bananas occurred to Louie as a gift to his parents
wringing memories, subtractions of the known.

Three cents of bananas beside him in the night
trolley, clustered like hot arcs of moonlight over worlds
of possibility, he must show Mama

and Papa. And he flew off the trolley car
while the enchanted bananas went home
with the conductor; it must have been a Monday.

*Never start anything on a Monday* he warned
fifty years hence, and you wanted to believe a
millionaire knows something the rest of us don't.

## V.   PEDDLER BOY: UNDERSTANDING LOUIE

Louie was a peddler boy
wending his way through stiff
Canadian streets

ingeniously. Grim November
was bonanza as he reconfigured
newspaper route into a company

of ten boys, a cart of berries
into a truck run, up and back
from Florida, and his big

Buick shone carmine in Ontario
spring. Beryl & Nellie still rocked silently
but now on chairs that crinkled plastic

wrap, *nouveau*. Louie delivered them rough
translations, a world left strange, unopened
as news rolled up, yellowing at the door.

## VI.  BLUE BASHA

After the library in Vancouver, under dark
of drizzle and doubtful wife, Moyshe
beguiled his Basha with Vaudeville,

Yiddish Theatre—a cultured life.
And home was noisy, fragrant
of another home gone: challah, honey, strife.

Basha developed a perilous
habit: a book a day. But a high
school scholar & daughter

of a junkman meant college
was anomalous, in vain.
Just a girl overheating

in June, Basha was shipped
summarily across the land
to hot-shot unread cousin Lou

who swooned maladroitly—
and she married him; it's said,
to dull the pain.

## VII. FURNITURE MOGUL

Louie's conquest was classic
Canadian, from London to Vancouver
he schlepped Basha & baby Bonnie

to give Moyshe a hand—in sales
of furniture, used. But Lou was used
to big getting huge, and the two blood

relations split over going factory
brand. Moyshe bet ten bucks: *Louie will
fold.* But Louie was the devil

who as you admired the brocade skirt
on a sofa would sell you the shirt
off your back, and the sofa

too, and an icebox
to keep the free gallon
of ice cream and your heart

racing after the sudden sale. *Bring in
a teacup, buy a mattress tax free*; his fever
was thrilling, self-made destiny.

## VIII.  DON'T FENCE ME IN

She is his
Betty Boop.
His bobble

bride. His
blond bookish
bomb,

banked and parsed
as subdivision
or Mondrian

as she looks down
upon herself, hard
as a paintbrush

unused, thin as a story
pressed under the
silver or softer

mink. Country club
connoisseur, golf & bridge
winner, tea-party doll.

In her stead, Basha taught
her three children and theirs
to read, study, think.

## IX.   STEAK & SEQUINS

Since the *shtetl* fear and money have risen
beneath him like a pot of porridge, out of control
and never enough. They ooze through his mouth

as if scorched by the journey. How can he help it:
pain makes us all rage in the key of F.

He would watch me swim laps by the hundreds,
count them off like husbands in waiting. To teach me
humility, he would stand me next to my beautiful mother.

Daddy provided steak and sequins;
the rest was up to me.

## X.   THE DEVELOPER

High-rise love.
Like an ad inscribed in the sky
with vapour crystals,

a disappearing
message, he named
each building

for a family child, or
whatever occurred in the gin
and tonic moment.

# XI.   PERCEPTION

Mama was a slim blonde in a red
T-Bird convertible with swept back
thoughts, and Dad perspired in plaid
suits the days of a big sale.

But my sister's parents were heroic,
audacious, bold. From the old world
to here, they were history.
They gave us our good lives.

Her grandparents faced the mean chill
of minority, their small Canadian home
fed her honeyed apple, pale lemon tea.
But the Bubba I adored

snored like a pachyderm, the eyelets
in her corset were cinched in ivory pairs,
and my Zeyde urged me night and day
to dream of Cadillacs.

My sister apprehends tradition
as lifeline cast from severity, from fleeing—
and here we are, soft as generations before us
could not dream—so that we could be free.

Yet I recall those before us feuded
over property and poodles,
the elders played pinochle in brocade
and lacy rooms, while my parents struck

little balls through vales emerald green
as palely I passed by. I remember
mother's affairs with books and
boys, and how my father knew

education was a trick: all free and guaranteed
on TV. Nevertheless my sister's parents
and their parents meet often with mine
in the stories we've been poured—

mixing there as fallen cherries
find earth in common, then soak
into fermented roots like ruby light
in tiny cups of Schnapps.

## XII.   DAD DYING

Whiskered and vague he's become
his own father, rocking and calculating
the body's swindle.

A king he once was from no money
down, a dollar in his shoe. From
Tchernovka to Pacific Hydrangea

Louie made himself. Now on top
blue pools of eye swivel from screen
to intruder, suspecting

the food on his plate. God is a doctor
who doesn't realize who is dying here
in this penthouse, how his pain

grows like a Tuesday investment.
*Never,* he once told me, *never be too proud
to pick up a penny.*

A billion pennies later, he lies on his
kingdom-sized bed, running from the
nickel and dime, the cloak-and-scythe

man, Louie is accelerating, his yellow
thumbnail pouncing on his channel-
changer like trap doors he once dreamed

up folded beneath a bed—the unsoiled
bed of a boy. This man's now on top but
bitter eyes glower above

thick-horned rims. They swivel from
intruder to screen, suspicious of the vast
family on his plate.

Then my father's dying in hospital,
his dogged sourness sweetening
towards oblivion. Such a flim-

flam thank-you ma'm
man, now my old man
is gone. The rich patternless

bruises decorating his limbs
like the torn coat of a toreador
gone too, cowed, caged, boxed

and delivered, the usual
deal—a lifetime
guarantee, expired.

# XIII.   LEGACY

a hospital ward in revelry
even the nurses are buoyant

as Basha surveys generations
bound by her, all four

no more Basha blue
now all tenderness

and wit opened out
with that future

thing: want
for the children

—better
than her clumsy start—

her lucent face
cirrus-capped as snow

the day she arrived
hazel eyes ablaze

as earth
will swallow

her, sated, beloved,
whole

# SIX

# DUSK, IF THAT

*to my mother, 1921–2007*

        Elsewhere
on earth, the shoeless    Pound, pound
Dust drinking up bloody feet    Even I have seen
rough alley, seen boulevard, dead shoes lone, telling
in the road    I've dwelt years in notorious
intersections of thought, and some danger

        But I'm safe now
and it's dusk, if that      Yet night burns
like a hobo — hands asleep on the rails    Something
going on in things grows indistinct    Mother:
vanished beginning    my tender source —

        On the wisteria, sun spark
And this salt face      Sky is tufting its feminine
hour, white on rose    Behind, the moon    smudged
        as errata

        I am the mare
moving dumbly up the tracks    I am the mouth
eating your words    Biting off
the sentence I'm no longer in:  Daughter.

# VIGIL

The operating theatre was studded with importance.
Five nations, their surgeons, and the message

*We care, we care too*
pumped, buoyed stupid hope.

The head of hands declared success
for his surgery, for the record.

But less of her
disembarked each rally, four

over six months. Days of
branch-infested winter light, spidery

with memories. Might the heart heal
itself? *Your mother is so*

*old,* so jello. The tissue had squatted
around her ventricle. They couldn't sew.

Still her jokes, hazel
eyes firing

among the combustible
confusions.

As the body cooled, she climbed
into my embrace.

Then the holy man is saying
*Don't worry—*

*it's just a body
in that box.*

# HAND ME DOWN

After the funeral, after the worn wall of faces confused to be grieving
next to the Original Cast of characters, and the children
clear-eyed and mound-leaping among the headstones,
after the rhythmic hands of the *Kaddish* deftly picking
at my secular lock, the seagulls following the procession
away like a boat, expecting like us to be fed; after all
this we return to living. We make love badly. Memory flips
its coin and rolls into a corner face-down.
Burnt-off cigarettes make a sluggish swirl
of bruises at the edge of the counter
afraid to leave the house wearing
these motherless hands.

# I DROWNED

This sea is the temperature of poured satin
translating the sun and its soothing semaphore
wave to wave, its brokelit dialect
as far as there is.
The last man I know gestures
absently, returns to his book, his towel, my fins
cast off in the sand like florescent lungs.

For now I am a maid of *mer*.
I am daddy's swimmer again, but
with breasts & several degrees.
My toes swoon me down as green pencilweed teases
at my ankles, then moves up behind, tails me
out; finally, alone.

Alone with the scalloped shore, littoral of urchin,
cowrie & anemone, all those dangerous secrets
aimed and silent, warlike, waving *adieu*? But still
so many bathers; I push from their gullous shouts
and laughs, farther, my torso finding its memory
of grace. Pulsing so effortlessly, I am riding the sea, riding
sleek as a sailfish on the back of a ray.

Off to the far right, Black Rock Point bolts
into the deep and the deep smashes
back, frosting its facets like arsenic.
All land is an interruption.

Angel & moon fish colour, orbit, and open
a path for me out and out. This is the parallel universe
the dolphins told of. This is where love
is plankton light, all around and within;
not shackle, bookend, stone.

And I am perfect dissolving.

Until breath finds no gills
in my length,
no length in my lungs

and Black Rock Point, too far,
too messy for hope
presses into the diamond second
that is my life.

       *Help*
*Her* I would cry
to the common set of limbs
passing nearby
as I myself thrust away ecstatic
into the great roil
of undertow, but *Help*
*Me* comes fast from

my warm blood thrum
& humanness, disappointing
all the watery world so
that I could tell
this to you now.

# LET'S SPRING

Winter has been a place
in Patagonia
where the ice is black.
But half-serious

in culottes, here's
spring with
her painted food
and dumpsters spilling

lavender wigs of
cellophane
to dust the cold
from our overwrought

ankles. Come,
Prima Vera. Crocuses
are brandishing their
little purple swords

at only you. Turn in
your animal-wear
for seersucker.
Remember soon will be

summer's numerous
hands,
your boyish spring hips
that submit.

Summer ideas
happen as cherry
grenade multiplicities, and
camp songs

will soon fill our throats
and bore them, but now
Five Hundred Bottles
of Beer would not be enough.

Before we know,
fall theatre season—
the drenched
marquees,

tragedies,
and all those pits.
But in spring
we recreate ourselves

as Mark Anthony, on Caesar
gone, prescribed it
to an earlier
confused throng.

JUICY

Sometimes I wish for it, a deluge
after drought, bombing the dust in my heart way up—

powdery asterisks of love. Sometimes I wish I were still juicy with that first boy.
Sometimes, out with the girls, I drink too much, rush to water's edge, feel salt

sea climbing up past my boots to where the woman first broke open. It's enough
then that on the streets the city burns high into cerulean night sky, drinking

stardust from the end of day. I remember one Egyptian lover, holding my hands
down as he blinded me with sex, and sometimes I want to borrow him for a brief

athletic hour from his sweeter, more suitable wife. Or that colossus from the east side
of town who visits, mounting the trembling stairway to my rooms, making love beside

the point of anything, hours on hours. Sometimes I feel wrapped
inside the letter that came from the original first boy. I'm spread long and teased

across a taffeta bed, kneesocks scissoring as I scan my Sartre, then Dali, for clues, why
no call, when Mother in pink golf attire tosses the letter onto some melting clock

in my book. *Sorry* limps at the end of his lettering.
I was a mess, like the ash streets after Mount St. Helens

blew her molten heart, then cooled, pocked
with broken air. Sometimes I know

there's no going back and sometimes I don't know
how anyone could not want

always to drink and eat peaches
under a plume of willow

where a boy once took you
far into clean, dusty summer.

# WHERE ENVELOPES COME FROM

*1977*

That curdled dead
horse smell coming

from machine jams
of paper and amber glue—

our Luddite knights,
horse & armor—

diminish the roar
insignificantly.

When all the machines are going
and they always are

it's all-the-machines-of-the-world
loud. A percussive shroud.

Or a hailstorm tumult
with birds running for cover

but we stay where we are
assigned. One grows accustomed.

The factory hangar holds us:
an enormous mouth

clamped shut, the chew
or swallow imminent.

It makes sense
over liquid lunch.

Some guys never sober up
till a strike is called—

then the harsher supervision
of their wives.

Our eyes raccoon
from sluggish shifts, short

stone-solid sleeps.
I dream about the factory

superintendent, he stands
behind me as I bend

and pour warm glue
into trays pooled inside

my machine—a colossal metal Fury
of a thing. He is a handsome

clean man, my nails are dark,
moonless, and my hands richly

paper-cut from tip to roughed-up
heel. I feel the machine in

me, how he and I could
climb into the vast dark side

of the hangar warehouse, into
the Meccano-set "stacks"

where one can cop
a smoke or, through denim

overalls, a feel. But I am here
in this place to beguile the proletariat.

I, the boat-rocking union
pinko chick. Popular

as a month of consecutive
Mondays.

Several two-men
sized women workers

rule the floor: huge, good
for "bumping" in what passes

for promotion. Their hard
eyes narrow, sink into their

sizeable faces if their stations
are threatened

and their mandibles
roil when sickness

or death open up
a coveted post.

Pillars of tree
remnants—

bleached, manila,
pastel—stand around us

like another species
tidy and doomed.

# APOLOGY

*Rwanda, 2009*

It's just that if you look at the world you get a stain
that won't come out—a kind of marbled beauty.
It's that the *genocidaire* was forgiven by the tall family.

It's that Earth is a vast dumb orb
of love and confusion, and time blows
and blows us its staccato kisses.

It's just that each of us begins as a female, then
gets on with it. It's that the great slow heron
swooped so near the apology in the village, the sun

searing its scar inside the sky; and at the tribunal
the elevator enclosed the rough moment
like a fast-action flower.

It's that justice is fragments dreaming
in full sentences, and the business
of the casualties

was analyzed closely,
never asking *What's the point*
*of the pond's reflection at moonless midnight?*

It's just that they make forgiveness hard
to believe, after all. After all—reply the living,
luminous in their cottons—all is glass, all belief.

# LAST WILL

My lone surviving
uncle drifts inside his suit-

days of verve, the big sales,
his name Sinatra or Vegas or

Sandwich. The family is un-naming
thickly around the festive

table. Yes, time does not curl
for us at the foot of the bed

listening for the leash to jangle,
and facts are particularly

tricky. Each morning there's
That Man on the street

with his coat of old
news, his diesel-hack knitting

the red of autumn. Another
man all dressed up in fatigues

incinerates a far-off enemy
from a suburban redoubt

in Langley, Virginia
by activating Predator Drones.

Yesterday's hit:
a funeral procession.

And fear just rolls
another cigarette.

Come, lie with me
in the big calm

beneath Canadian skies.
Sorrow will not vanish

without our gaze.
Let's study geese awhile

instead, their pretty incident
of arrow. Come,

have a seat in my
embrace, discuss the kismet

of our good fortune. Sincerely,
your most humble
    —Executrix

# NOTES

"A Brief History of the Blues" was inspired by R. Crumb's *Heroes of Blues, Jazz & Country*.

"Enter the Chudnovsky Brothers" was based on "Art and Science Rubric" in *The New Yorker* for April 11, 2005, about the *Unicorn Tapestries* restoration project at The Cloisters.

"Teacups & Mink" became the script for a film of the same title. It is also the text for a limited series of original art books (artist Bonnie Leyton) that are touring as part of a multimedia art show which debuted in Vancouver in Dec–Jan 2008 and next appeared in St. John's, Newfoundland, in March 2010. The film has garnered awards for Best International Short, Poetic Genre & Best Directorial Debut from the New York Independent International Film & Video Festival 2008 and Best Short at the Desert Falls Film Festival 2008 and was also screened at the St. John's Women's Film Festival, 2009.

"Last Will" refers to predator drone activity, drawn from *The New Yorker*, October 26, 2009, "The Predator War" by Jane Mayer. The article describes the incident of an air strike in Afghanistan, in which between 75 and 125 people were mistaken for Taliban insurgents. The bomb strike left such a tangle of bodies that village elders resorted to handing pieces of unidentifiable corpses to the grieving families. One Afghan villager said, "I took a piece of flesh home and called it my son."

# ACKNOWLEDGEMENTS

"A Thing Past," *Prism International*, fall 2009.

"Speaking in the Ventricular," *The Smoking Poet*, winter 2009.

"My Youth Machine-rolled, Smoked to Its Stub," *ByWords Quarterly Journal*, 2008; honourable mention, John Newlove Poetry Award, 2009; *Descant*, Writers in Prison issue, fall 2010.

"A Tool I Can Say With," *CV2*, fall 2009.

"Changing Channels," *CV2*, 2007.

"Slim Evidence of Dubious Quality," *Court Green*, Columbia College, Chicago, winter 2010.

"Taste of City," *Poetry New Zealand*, 2009.

"Unsexy," finalist, Burnaby Writers' Society contest, 2007; *Dalhousie Review*, 2009.

"To the Lighthouse," *CV2*, 2007, and selected for *The Best Canadian Poetry in English 2008*.

"Darwin is Despondent," *Court Green*, Columbia College, Chicago, fall 2007.

"A Brief History of the Blues," *ByWords Quarterly Journal*, 2009.

"Big," *Mi Poesias*, New York, 2007.

"Projection," *The Fiddlehead*, 2009.

"Trans Canada Drowning, Summer '96," from *Love in the Media Age* anthology, 1999.

"Beached," finalist, Burnaby Writers' Society Poetry Contest, 2007.

"Cuba, Por Fin!," *MiPOesias*, New York, 2007.

"Mediations Across the Table," selected for *Seven Deadly Sins* anthology, 2007.

"Enter the Chudnovsky Brothers," *Dream Catcher* 23, Canadian Issue, UK, 2009.

"Poster Child," *Court Green*, Columbia College, Chicago, winter 2010.

"Saffron," *Arabesque*, Tangiers-Paris, 2007.

"Rowing Lesson #9: Getting Out of Bed," *Poetry London*, 2009.

"Teacups & Mink" is the script for a film of the same title (see Notes).

"Dusk, If That," *Descant*, spring 2010.

"Where Envelopes Come From," *MiPOesiass*, New York, 2007.

"Apology," *CV2*, "The Keystone of Canadian Poetry Turns 35" issue, fall 2010.

# GRATITUDE

I wish to thank Roo Borson for her meticulous, intelligent editorial involvement in this manuscript; The New School in New York where this manuscript was begun as part of a Master's thesis; and, in particular, the counsel of David Lehman and the scholarly instruction of Mark Bibbins. Thanks to my children James & Joseph Corcoran and my sister Bonnie Leyton who support me steadfastly in my work; to Karen Hildebrand and Barbara Shuman who any time I asked gave feedback, drawing me from my cave to take a fresh look; and to my publisher, Tightrope Books, for having faith in this manuscript.

# ABOUT THE AUTHOR

Leanne Averbach is a Canadian poet and filmmaker. She has been published and has performed with musicians across Canada, in the US, and in Italy. Her first book, *Fever* (Mansfield Press), was shortlisted for the Gerald Lampert Memorial Award in 2006. Her companion CD *Fever* is a fusion of her spoken words and the blues/jazz accompaniment of the Vancouver group Indigo. Averbach's second short film based on her poetry, *Teacups & Mink*, has garnered numerous awards. For more information visit www.leanneaverbach.com.

FOR THE LOVE
OF POETRY

www.TightropeBooks.com